Reader's Guides

SECOND SERIES 11

HISTORICAL FICTION

Introduction by
ALFRED DUGGAN

Reading list compiled by
W. A. TAYLOR

T0345984

PUBLISHED FOR
THE NATIONAL BOOK LEAGUE
AT THE UNIVERSITY PRESS
CAMBRIDGE
1957

CAMBRIDGE UNIVERSITY PRESS
Cambridge, New York, Melbourne, Madrid, Cape Town,
Singapore, São Paulo, Delhi, Mexico City

Cambridge University Press
The Edinburgh Building, Cambridge CB2 8RU, UK

Published in the United States of America by Cambridge University Press, New York

www.cambridge.org
Information on this title: www.cambridge.org/9781107622135

© Cambridge University Press 1957

First published 1957
Re-issued 2013

A catalogue record for this publication is available from the British Library

ISBN 978-1-107-62213-5 Paperback

CONTENTS

INTRODUCTION

The Novel is a comparatively new form of art, and th historical novel quite a recent development. In the Middle Ages, and even more during the Renaissance, some writers placed their stories of high life in remote countries or distant epochs; but they made no attempt to depict the appropriate manners and customs—the court of King Lear is like any Tudor court, and *Rasselas, Prince of Abyssinia*, discusses in his happy valley the behaviour of eighteenth-century St. James's. The advantage gained by an unfamiliar setting was that the reader could not anticipate the outcome of the plot, and that melodramatic changes of fortune seemed less implausible.

By the middle of the eighteenth century writers were beginning to be interested in the queer goings-on of their ancestors. This was especially true of Britain, where the Reformation had brought great changes in everyday life, so that every shire was littered with the remains of mighty buildings now become superfluous. It was the strangeness of the age of chivalry which first attracted the interest of the polite. In Horace Walpole's *Castle of Otranto* anything might happen, and nearly everything did. Monks, nuns, knights and magicians are seen as equally strange, each moved by motives equally incomprehensible to a civilised man. Walpole's imitators, writing in the particular genre of the Gothick Tale, were out to shock, not to convince.

But in one corner of Britain the age of chivalry lingered on until 1746. Walter Scott might talk to old men who had seen Rob Roy; *The Heart of Midlothian* and *The Antiquary* depict a world which had only recently passed over the horizon. In his Scottish stories, therefore, Sir Walter set himself to recount the remarkable adventures of ordinary men, men like his fellow-citizens in the Edinburgh of 1800, who happened to live in a different kind of civilisation.

Thus early were formed the two main branches of the historical novel. Horace Walpole, and his imitators in their Gothick Tales, delighted in the absurd inconsequence of knight-errantry and necromancy. Scott understood that to a burgess of Glasgow a Highland paladin might be merely a tiresome obstacle to commerce. From the *Castle of Otranto* descend all the wild tales of desperate deeds which go so well into Cinemascope, the Ruritanian adventures in which every actor is of royal blood, and, at a greater remove from the original source, the White Queens reigning in Central Africa and the ingenuities of space-fiction. All these depend for their charm (and the best of them possess great charm) on the postulate that our ancestors, or races living at a great distance from this country, are not a bit like us.

From the second source we get, at the end of a long descent, the stories of Robert Graves and Naomi Mitchison. These make their effect (to me one of the strongest effects in modern letters) by assuming that men and women fundamentally like us once conducted their lives under very different conditions. This second stream seems to me the more worthy of notice. Let us try to map its course.

At the beginning we note that Walter Scott composed his novels within two different frameworks. When he was writing the Civil Wars and their Jacobite epilogue were almost contemporary politics—as they are still contemporary politics in Belfast. By taking pains he could reconstruct his setting with perfect accuracy, and he took the pains. The dialect is correct, so are the details of daily life, money, eating and drinking, and especially religion. The reader is placed in a concrete and convincing environment.

Scott's tales of the Middle Ages breathe a different atmosphere. For one thing, though he could see the good in both

Covenanters and Cavaliers, to him the idea of a grown man dedicating his life to prayer and self-denial was so absurd that he made no effort to understand a monk. He neglected not only the technicalities of Popery, bringing a friar into *Ivanhoe* fifty years before St. Francis and, of course, walling up an erring nun in *The Abbot*, but also the influence of religion on the ordinary layman. If he had stopped to think he must have seen that a Scotsman would not ride all the way to Palestine unless he felt pretty strongly about the fate of the Holy Places; but his Crusaders in *The Talisman* feel no more hatred of the infidel than if they were engaged on opposite sides in a Test Match.

This misconception of the mind of the Middle Ages seems to me much more important than any number of mistakes about the date of the first stone castle or the rules of the twelfth-century tournament. But Sir Walter wrote for a public that knew nothing of the Middle Ages.

However, there was another period, besides the Stuart past, on which the eighteenth-century public was well-informed. Dr. Johnson and his friends knew a great deal more about Roman Emperors than about Plantagenet Kings. The story of the true historical novel is the story of the expansion of these two patches of knowledge; until nowadays, except for a wisp of fog in the Dark Ages, any period of English history, from Julius Caesar to the present day, may be used as a background for a tale of fiction, the author assuming a certain co-operation from the educated reader.

In the nineteenth century this was not so. Bulwer-Lytton provides a good example. *The Last Days of Pompeii* gives an accurate picture of its times, *The Last of the Barons* does not. Lytton wrote for a public who had read Tacitus and Pliny, but who knew no more of the fifteenth century than they could find in Shakespeare and Holinshed.

With slightly more knowledge, the mid-Victorians remained quite sure that their own point of view was the point of view of the ordinary man in any age. Kingsley's *Hypatia* is an example of a good story spoiled, at least for some readers, by the intrusion of an historically false outlook. Kingsley had the letters of Synesius to guide him, and all his historical facts are accurate; but his Goths are just nineteenth-century Germans of the progressive kind, instead of the tiresome savages they seemed to the average Roman. In *Westward Ho !* he gave free rein to his hatred of Popery and Spain; this book ,which is still sometimes given as a prize to schoolboys, teaches that in dealing with Irishmen and other disgusting foreigners an English hero need consider himself bound neither by the Ten Commandments nor by the ordinary code of honour. Above all, Kingsley missed the important points that Elizabethan England was something new, defiant of the rest of Christendom; he seems to consider that Philip of Spain was an aggressor, attacking harmless innocents who had lived since time immemorial under an Anglican settlement.

By the 1890's the scene is changing. The new history schools at Oxford and Cambridge are diffusing a true picture of the past; the Master of the Rolls is publishing our mediaeval chronicles as they were written; Pepys, the Verneys, the Pastons, are becoming known. Thackeray's *Esmond* and Dickens's *Tale of Two Cities* had been projections of current affairs into the past. Thackeray could draw a Jacobite by looking at any old-fashioned Tory who deplored the Reform Bill; Dickens saw the Reign of Terror reflected in the revolutions of 1830 and 1848. The landmark is Stevenson's *The Black Arrow.* Using the Paston Letters, Stevenson got right away from the wellknown main stream of history, to write about private individuals of the fifteenth century as they really were. It is not the best of his books, but in some ways it is the most important thing he ever wrote.

Now we come to writers who seem to me contemporary, because their books were still "current fiction" when I read them as a schoolboy. Conan Doyle took more trouble over *Sir Nigel* and *The White Company* than over any of his detective stories, and regarded the writing of them as his most important work. He followed Froissart for public events, and Jusserand's *Wayfaring Life in Mediaeval England* for local colour, and got all his facts absolutely accurate. The result was two very fine stories, but they are not really placed in the fourteenth century; the hero, and all the other sympathetic characters, talk and feel like progressive late-Victorians; Conan Doyle never tried to think himself into the skin of a fourteenth-century knight.

At the beginning of the twentieth century there were plenty of good historical novels. But most of them showed the past as a queer though fascinating peepshow, teaching the moral that in those days people were very odd; all except the hero, who is usually as up-to-date as the *Daily Mail*. Marjorie Bowen, who wrote some of her best work under the pseudonym of George Preedy, sometimes made the past come alive. But when she does this she becomes too excited by the appalling goings-on of the Middle Ages. *The Viper of Milan* and *The Sword Decides* deal with ordinary Italian thuggery, which can be paralleled in more recent times; under Miss Bowen's treatment the casual murders and treasons seem more terrible than anything that happened to the House of Atreus.

H. C. Bailey, better known as a writer of detective stories, produced in *The Fool* a fine picture of the young Henry II; in *The Sea Captain* he explored the obscure subject of galley-warfare in the Mediterranean, otherwise neglected except by Rafael Sabatini. But though these are exciting tales of adventure, to me they do not ring true as genuine

9

pictures of the past. Any reader must feel that they could only have been written by an Edwardian author who had views on tariff reform and the powers of the House of Lords.

Gilbert Parker and Mary Johnstone had founded the tradition of the American historical romance, where accuracy in a setting of the recent past is the factor most sought after. Again, their characters are too modern. As a child I first learned about the inflation of currency from reading one of Mary Johnstone's heroes regret, with marvellous foresight, the consequences of Confederacy's reckless printing of paper dollars. A neglected work in this field is Owen Wister's *The Virginian*, which shows the frontier in all its beastliness, as seen by a civilised American. It is a good corrective to the modern adulation of the gunman.

To me, the real eye-opener, showing what could be done with the historical novel, was Naomi Mitchison's *The Conquered*. Here was a Gallic boy of the first century B.C., thinking and behaving as such; he even works magic, to his own satisfaction, instead of being progressively anticlerical about Druids. But this came after the great watershed of modern times, the War of 1914. Earlier, Stanley Weyman and Maurice Hewlett had written as though they regretted that their contemporaries no longer carried swords; we know, to our loss, what a bore it is to be compelled to carry a tommy-gun.

Before Naomi Mitchison I can think of only one historical novelist who genuinely thought himself into the past—Ford Madox Hueffer in *Ladies Whose Bright Eyes*. Even he cheated a little, by making his hero a modern publisher, miraculously carried back to the fourteenth century; but the people his hero meets are thoroughly convincing.

After Naomi Mitchison the names come thick and fast. Whether it was that she set a fashion, or merely that *The Conquered* was published while others were already at work, since then historical novels have altered completely, and for the better. Robert Graves has made us see the reality behind Roman history and C. S. Forester, writing for a generation that has heard gunfire, makes us smell black powder. (I myself prefer his tales of campaigning on land, *The Gun* and *Death to the French*, to all the seadoggishness of Hornblower; but I know myself in a minority).

Evan John is dead, after writing one or two fine crusading stories. But at present Zoé Oldenbourg, H. M. Prescott, Margaret Irwin and Edith Simon are still writing. I recommend their works—and, of course, those of the authors mentioned in the text above. They show us not only how our ancestors fought and made love, but how they thought and what they believed. That seems to me the only justification for the writing of historical novels.

ALFRED DUGGAN

MENTIONED IN THE INTRODUCTION

JOHNSON, SAMUEL. *Rasselas, Prince of Abyssinia* (1759) O.U.P.*

WALPOLE, HORACE. *The Castle of Otranto* (1764) Grey Walls Press 1950.*

SCOTT, Sir WALTER. *Rob Roy* (1818); *The Heart of Midlothian* (1886); *The Antiquary* (1816); *Ivanhoe* (1820); *The Abbot* (1820); *The Talisman* (1888); Collins New Classics, 5s. 6d., 5s.

BULWER-LYTTON, Lord LYTTON. *The Last Days of Pompeii* (1834)· Collins New Classics, 5s. 6d.; *The Last of the Barons* (1843).

KINGSLEY, CHARLES. *Hypatia* (1853); *Westward Ho!* (1855). Dent (Everyman) 8s. 6d.

THACKERAY, W. M. *Henry Esmond* (1852). O.U.P. (World's Classics) 6s. Dent (Everyman) 7s. Collins New Classics, 5s. 6d.

DICKENS, CHARLES. *A Tale of Two Cities* (1859). O.U.P. (World's Classics) 5s. Dent (Everyman) 6s.

STEVENSON, R. L. *The Black Arrow* (1888). Collins New Classics, 5s. 6d.

DOYLE, Sir ARTHUR CONAN. *Sir Nigel* (1906); *The White Company* (1916). Murray, each 8s. 6d.

BOWEN, MARJORIE. *The Viper of Milan* (1917); *The Sword Decides* (1908).

BAILEY, H. C. *The Fool.* Methuen, 1921. *The Sea Captain.* Methuen, 1916.

WISTER, OWEN. *The Virginian.* Macmillan, 1919.

HUEFFER, FORD MADOX (later Ford Madox Ford). *Ladies Whose Bright Eyes.* Constable, 1920.

MITCHISON, NAOMI. *The Conquered* (see No. 160 below).

FORESTER, C. S. *Death to the French; The Gun* (see Nos. 73, 75).

*Included in *Shorter Novels of the Eighteenth Century.* Dent (Everyman) 6s.

READING LIST

Taking the 'watershed' of the First World War as a starting point, this list includes only novels published between 1923 and the end of 1956. Historical accuracy has been a criterion for inclusion. All publishers are London firms except where otherwise stated. Prices (net and subject to alteration) are those prevailing in January, 1957, and are given only where a book is known to be available new as this list goes to press. Many of the books out of print can still be obtained secondhand and from public libraries.

1. ALLEN, HERVEY. *Action at Aquila.* Gollancz, 1938.

The American Civil War is dealt with here in rather less space than the author needed for the Napoleonic era, in his first novel; but the stage is equally crowded and the book never lacks lively incident.

2. —— *Anthony Adverse.* Gollancz, 1934; now Heinemann. 25s.

A remarkable achievement, covering the entire Napoleonic era through the life and death of the hero, who gives his name to the book. There are many good things in the twelve hundred pages, but only those readers with uncommon stamina will refrain from a little judicious skipping.

3. —— *The Forest and the Fort.* Heinemann, 1943.

4. —— *Bedford Village.* Heinemann, 1945.

These two novels, set in the forests and mountains of Pennsylvania at the time of the Seven Years' War, show once again the author's fondness for a large canvas, a profusion of incident and a multiplicity of characters. The central figure is Salathiel Albine, who as a child was kidnapped by an Indian Chief.

5. ALMEDINGEN, E. M. *Fair Haven.* Hutchinson, 1956.

An English name on a tombstone in a neglected cemetery in St. Petersburg (now Leningrad) inspired this story of the craftsmen and labourers who came from all the countries of Western Europe to create Peter the Great's 'city built on bones'.

6. —— *The Lion of the North.* Constable, 1938.

Imagination is stronger than history in this fictional account of that enigmatic monarch, Charles XII of Sweden. But the background is accurate and there is a vivid picture of the march into Russia in the depths of winter, from which Hitler might have derived a lesson or two.

13

7. —— *Stephen's Light.* Hutchinson, 1956. 12*s*. 6*d*.

This novel of fifteenth-century Germany takes its title from the house of a rich merchant, whose daughter is the heroine. A simple plot enables the author to concentrate on the everyday life of the time—the gossip of the market place and tavern.

8. —— *Young Catherine.* Constable, 1937.

The life of Catherine the Great, from childhood to her proclamation as Empress, portrayed in a thoroughly successful novel.

9. Asch, Sholem. *The Apostle.* Macdonald, 1949. 17*s*. 6*d*.

The Apostle is, of course, Paul; and the author is entirely at home in the period.

10. —— *Mary.* Macdonald, 1950. 15*s*.

This is, in effect, a re-writing of the Four Gospels as a life of the Virgin Mary.

11. —— *The Nazarene.* Routledge, 1939. 15*s*.

The most difficult of all subjects for the historical novelist, handled with great artistry through the medium of three eye-witnesses.

12. —— *The Prophet.* Macdonald, 1956. 16*s*.

The hero of this powerful novel is Isaiah, the prophet, at the end of the Babylonian captivity, and the author paints a vivid picture of the Jewish nation in exile.

13. Ashton, Helen. *William and Dorothy.* Collins, 1938. 7*s*. 6*d*.

William and Dorothy Wordsworth, and Coleridge—'three people with one soul'—are brought to life in this successful piece of fictional biography, carefully concocted from Dorothy's journals and letters, and other documentary evidence.

14. Austin, F. Britten. *The Road to Glory.* Thornton Butterworth, 1935.

15. —— *Forty Centuries Look Down.* Thornton Butterworth, 1936.

Two connected works which between them give an account of the early career of Napoleon—the young General Bonaparte's Italian and Egyptian campaigns, 1796–8.

16. Bacchelli, Riccardo. *The Mill on the Po.* Hutchinson, 1952. 15*s*.

This famous Italian novel of the Risorgimento has been beautifully translated. The millers of the Po, with their water-wheels hung from barges, were renowned for their independence, and Lazzaro Scacerni was of this breed. Every aspect of the rise of Italy in the nineteenth century is set forth by means of well-drawn, living characters, in an outstanding book. The chronicle of the Scacerni family is continued up to the First World War in *Nothing New under the Sun*, Hutchinson, 1955. 8s. 6d.

17. BARING, MAURICE. *Robert Peckham*. Heinemann, 1930.

With delicate grace the author depicts the spiritual conflicts of a Tudor Englishman whose devotion to the Catholic faith is his prime concern. Drama in plenty is provided by Henry VIII's religious policy, the plots of the reign of Mary and the triumph of the Reformers under Queen Elizabeth.

18. BARON, ALEXANDER. *The Golden Princess*. Cape, 1954. 15s.

An excellent tale of Marina, the Indian girl who was interpreter and concubine to Cortes. Her half-Indian, half-Spanish mind is subtly explored.

19. BEACH, MRS. HICKS. *A Cardinal of the Medici*. C.U.P., 1937.

The cardinal is Ippolito de Medici, but the book is more than a life of this vivid Renaissance figure; it is a penetrating excursion into the whole exciting and dangerous world of sixteenth-century Italy, which does full justice to the magnificence of its subject.

20. BELL, NEIL. *The Abbot's Heel*. Collins, 1939.

A most successful attempt to portray the mood and manners of fourteenth-century England, just before the Black Death. The main theme is the attempt of the rising anti-feudal groups to shake off the supremacy of the Church and nobility.

21. BENGTSSON, FRANS G. *The Long Ships*. Collins, 1954. 15s. and 3s. 6d.

This story of a tenth-century Viking reads like a genuine saga of the Dark Ages. The author, who is a Swedish poet and man of letters, shows a superb understanding of the Norsemen of that remote period.

22. BENTLEY, PHYLLIS. *Freedom, Farewell*. Gollancz, 1936.

A stylish and learned account of the career of Julius Caesar.

23. —— *Take Courage*. Gollancz, 1940.

The setting is Bradford and Yorkshire, during the Civil War.

15

It is a somewhat hackneyed theme—homely Roundhead versus gay Cavalier for the hand of the lady—but the background of the vital issues of politics and religion is well done.

24. BORDEN, MARY. *The King of the Jews.* Heinemann, 1935.

The author re-tells the familiar story with such passion, sincerity and conviction that she makes it as gripping as if it were new to us.

25. —— *Mary of Nazareth.* Heinemann, 1933.

This study of the Mother of Jesus is triumphantly successful.

26. BOWEN, MARJORIE. *Dickon.* Hodder, 1929.

Makes an interesting comparison with Carola Oman's *Crouchback* since it is the story of Richard III from the pro-Yorkist angle. To Miss Bowen, Richard was the king who could do no wrong, who was dogged by undeserved misfortune.

27. —— *Exchange Royal.* Hutchinson, 1940.

The author is in her favourite period—the late seventeenth century. The plot derives from the intrigues which surrounded the invitation to William of Orange to take the English throne; and the central figure is that of Edmund Tornier, a spy in the service of James II. The story is continued into the reign of William of Orange in *Today is Mine*, Hutchinson, 1941.

28. BRIGGS, K. M. *Hobberdy Dick.* Eyre & Spottiswoode, 1955. 12*s.* 6*d.*

A fascinating book by a learned anthropologist. The period is the mid-seventeenth century, and the events of the story are seen through the eyes of Lar, the tutelary spirit of a Cotswold Manor house, whose servitude began when the first Stone Age farmers came to the Costswolds.

29. BROPHY, JOHN. *Gentleman of Stratford.* Collins, 1939.

None other, of course, than Will Shakespeare. An eminent bookman has described this as 'perhaps the best novel ever written in which the chief character is Shakespeare.'

30. BROSTER, D. K. *Child Royal.* Heinemann, 1937.

Mary, Queen of Scots, from an unusual aspect—that of her happy childhood in France.

31. —— *Flight of the Heron.* Heinemann, 1925. 8*s.* 6*d.*

32. —— *The Gleam in the North.* Heinemann, 1927. 8*s.* 6*d.*

33. —— *The Dark Mile*. Heinemann, 1929. 8*s*. 6*d*.

A rousing and well-woven trilogy of the '45 and the Highlands in the eighteenth century. It is rich in local colour and admirably embroidered with historical detail. The account of Culloden and the work of ' Butcher ' Cumberland and his men is horrifying.

34. —— *Ships in the Bay*. Heinemann, 1931. 8*s*. 6*d*.

Those who believe that the last invasion of this island was in 1066 should read this account of the landing of the French at Fishguard in 1797.

35. BRYHER (pseud.). *The Fourteenth of October*. Collins, 1954. 10*s*. 6*d*.

A most distinguished piece of writing, which tells the adventures of Wulf, the son of an eleventh-century Yorkshire landowner.

36. —— *Roman Wall*. Collins, 1955. 10*s*. 6*d*.

The story of a few days in the lives of people living near the Rhenish frontier of Switzerland in the time of the Emperor Gallienus. Unobtrusively the mood of the period is built up in the reader's mind—the surface appearance of complacency, disturbed by waves of fear and despair.

37. BUCK, PEARL S. *Imperial Woman*. Methuen, 1956. 16*s*.

Tzu Hsi rose from being one among scores of concubines to become the last Empress of the Manchus. Her long life makes a fascinating story.

38. BYRNE, DONN. *Brother Saul*. Sampson Low, 1927.

Not all historians will agree with this interpretation of the Roman Empire at the beginning of the Christian era; but the Apostle Paul and the other characters are real people, not two-dimensional figures.

39. —— *The Power of the Dog*. Sampson Low, 1929.

The central figure is Lord Castlereagh, and although he is depicted rather vaguely the book contains some brilliant vignettes of other great figures of the period: Nelson, Canning, Wordsworth, Shelley, Goethe, etc.

40. CALDWELL, TAYLOR. *The Earth is the Lord's*. Collins, 1941.

A skilful reconstruction of the early life of Genghis Khan, when he was engaged in his preliminary task of uniting the scattered Mongol tribes.

41. CHARQUES, DOROTHY. *Time's Harvest.* Hamish Hamilton, 1940; now Murray. 10*s.* 6*d.*

The story opens in 1830, when the personal relationship between man and master was dissolving and was being replaced by abstracts such as 'Worker' and 'Capitalist'.

42. CHILD, PHILIP. *Village of Souls.* Thornton Butterworth, 1933.

A story of French Canada in 1665, which did not get the attention it deserved. The author imparts to his tale imagination, human warmth of feeling and a remarkable vitality.

43. CLOETE, STUART. *Turning Wheels.* Collins, 1937. Cheap edn. 1955. 2*s.* 6*d.*

A novel of the Great Trek, when the migration had been in progress for fifteen years and the River Vaal had been crossed.

44. COLLINGWOOD, W. G. *The Bondwomen.* Heinemann, 1932.

A historical novel by a historian, dealing with a period shunned by most historical novelists—the Norse invasion of the tenth century.

45. —— *Thorstein of the Mere.* Heinemann, 1929.

The hero is the younger son of Swain, chief of the Norsemen living in Lakeland in the tenth century. Written in a simple,direct style, it has many similarities to the Norse Sagas. It lifts a corner of the veil that hangs over an obscure and confused period in our national history.

46. COOPER, LETTICE U. *Good Venture.* Hodder, 1928.

A story of the Merchant Adventurers of England and the fight for the independence of the Netherlands against the tyranny of Spain, maintains a nice balance between fiction and history. The characters move against a strictly accurate historical background, but they never degenerate into puppets.

47. CRONYN, GEORGE W. *The Fool of Venus.* Cape, 1934.

A gigantic novel of twelfth-century Europe. The hero is Peire Vidal, the celebrated troubadour, but the book lives in the memory for its brilliant picture of the enthusiasm, energy and waste of the Fourth Crusade. It is not easy reading, but it is very rewarding.

48. —— *Mermaid Tavern.* Jarrolds, 1938.

The life of Christopher Marlowe, by a writer who knows his way about Elizabethan London and faithfully portrays the swash-buckling and coarseness of its life.

49. CROZIER, W. P. *The Fates are Laughing.* Cape, 1945.

The story of two aristocratic Roman families under the early Roman emperors. A lifetime's leisure from journalism was spent on this book, and the result is a triumph.

50. DANE, CLEMENCE. *The Moon is Feminine.* Heinemann, 1938.

A brilliant picture of Regency Brighton, as a setting for the career of Henry Cope—the 'Green Man' who dressed entirely in green and ate only green food.

51. DARK, ELEANOR. *The Timeless Land.* Collins, 1941.

The beginnings of the Australian nation, told with great vividness in a most memorable novel.

52. DE WOHL, LOUIS. *The Restless Flame.* Gollancz, 1952.

The life of St. Augustine of Hippo, narrated with historical accuracy and a genuine understanding of the period—the time when Christianity had recently become the official religion of the Empire.

53. DELVES-BROUGHTON, J. *Crown Imperial.* Faber, 1949.

An imaginative, but not fanciful, biography of Queen Elizabeth. It paints a convincing picture of her single-minded devotion to her people.

54. DIX, TENNILLE. *The Black Baron.* Nash & Grayson, 1931.

The 'thrillerish' title hides a first-class account of the extraordinary career of Gilles de Rais, the strangest of the Marshals of fifteenth-century France.

55. D'OYLEY, ELIZABETH. *The Mired Horse.* M. Joseph, 1951.

Thomas Howard, Duke of Norfolk, bogged down in the Ridolfi plot. The background shows evidence of wide reading in the period, and there are brilliant pictures of the vain busybody Ridolfi and of a Tudor state trial.

56. DRUON, MAURICE. *The Iron King.* Hart-Davis, 1956. 15s.

The Iron King is Philip IV of France (Philip the Fair). The book has all the drama, colour, sensuality and barbarism of the Middle Ages. It is one of the best historical novels of recent years.

57. —— *The Strangled Queen.* Hart-Davis, 1956. 15s.

The second in a series of novels which the author plans under the title *The Accursed Kings.* This successor to *The Iron King* tells the story of the conflict between Philip's son, Louis X, supported by the great Marigny, and Charles of Valois, Philip's brother.

19

58. DUGGAN, ALFRED. *Conscience of the King.* Faber, 1951. 12s. 6d.

The story is told through the medium of an old man who, in describing the events of his life, puts together a picture of the founding of Wessex. The author, an archaeologist, asserts that all the facts in the book are supported by history, but admits that his interpretation of them may not be unanimously accepted.

59. —— *God and my Right.* Faber, 1955. 15s.

The hero is Thomas à Becket. The author shows tremendous knowledge of his subject, and of the background of the period.

60. —— *Knight with Armour.* Faber, 1950. 12s. 6d.

A straightforward novel of the First Crusade, which contains interesting information on war-horses and armour.

61. —— *The Lady for Ransom.* Faber, 1953. 15s.

The historical career of Roussel of Bailleul, the Norman knight who fought the Turks in the middle of the eleventh century, told in a distinguished novel which gives a brilliant impression of the period and does not gloss over its coarseness and brutality.

62. —— *Leopards and Lilies.* Faber, 1954. 12s. 6d.

A genuine contribution to our understanding of thirteenth-century English history.

63. —— *The Little Emperors.* Faber, 1951. 15s.

The collapse of Roman rule in Britain between A.D. 405 and 412.

64. —— *Winter Quarters.* Faber, 1956. 15s.

Mr. Duggan's latest novel relates the story of Camus, a young Gaul, who enlists in the Roman cavalry, obtains promotion and goes to Rome in the service of Publius Crassus.

65. DUKE, WINIFRED. *King of the Highland Hearts.* W. & R. Chambers, 1929.

Charles Edward's career after the disaster of Culloden, told with strict impartiality.

66. FAST, HOWARD. *Citizen Tom Paine.* Bodley Head, 1945.

Fictional biography, but two-thirds of the novel is concerned with the War of Independence, and there are forceful studies of the great figures of the American Revolution.

67. —— *Freedom Road.* Bodley Head, 1947.

A sincere and deeply moving novel of South Carolina in the '70s, where a mixed community of negro and white was formed and subsequently brought to a violent end by the Ku Klux Klan.

68. FEUCHTWANGER, LEON. *Josephus.* Secker, 1932.

69. —— *The Jew of Rome.* Hutchinson, 1935.

70. —— *The Day Will Come.* Hutchinson, 1942.

A tremendously ambitious account of the life and times of Josephus. The canvas is vast, but all the characters, from the Emperor to the little Jewish glassblowers, are depicted 'in the round'.

71. FISHER, VARDIS. *Children of God.* Methuen, 1940.

The history of the Mormons, told in great detail, from the boyhood of Joseph Smith to the last attempt to settle in Mexico, after being driven from Utah.

72. FORD, FORD MADOX. *A Little Less Than Gods.* Duckworth, 1928.

Napoleon on Elba, and the hectic period of the 'Hundred Days'.

73. FORESTER, C. S. *Death to the French.* Bodley Head, 1932. Penguin, 1955. 2s. 6d.

The Peninsular War, with a simple Sussex infantryman, named Dodd, waging a one-man guerilla struggle.

74. —— *The Earthly Paradise.* M. Joseph, 1940. 12s. 6d. and 4s. 6d.

An account of the third voyage of Columbus, which ended in his humiliation and disgrace.

75. —— *The Gun.* Bodley Head, 1933. 6s. Penguin, 1955. 2s. 6d.

A dramatic story of the Spanish guerillas who carried on the fight against Napoleon after the defeat of their country.

76. —— *Mr. Midshipman Hornblower.* M. Joseph, 1950. 12s. 6d. and 4s. 6d.

77. —— *Lieutenant Hornblower.* M. Joseph, 1952. 12s. 6d. and 4s. 6d.

78. —— *Hornblower and the 'Atropos'.* M. Joseph, 1953. 12s. 6d. and 5s.

21

79. —— *The Happy Return*. M. Joseph, 1937. 12*s*. 6*d*., 6*s*. and
4*s*. 6*d*.

80. —— *A Ship of the Line*. M. Joseph, 1938, 12*s*. 6*d*., 6*s*. and
4*s*. 6*d*.

81. —— *Flying Colours*. M. Joseph, 1938. 12*s*. 6*d*., 6*s*. and 4*s*. 6*d*.

82. —— *The Commodore*. M. Joseph, 1945. 12*s*. 6*d*. and 4*s*. 6*d*.

83. —— *Lord Hornblower*. M. Joseph, 1946. 12*s*. 6*d*., 6*s*. and
4*s*. 6*d*.

This series of novels about the Royal Navy of Nelson's era might
well be sub-titled ' From Carronade to Coronet'. They are uneven
in quality, but the best of them contain a wealth of authentic
detail about the Navy during one of its most glorious epochs.
Nos. 76-83 are available from Penguin Books, each 2*s*. 6*d*.

84. FRASER, SIR RONALD. *Flight of Wild Geese*. Cape, 1955.
13*s*. 6*d*.

The setting is China under the Sung emperors, and in a witty and
graceful story the author makes the China of this period appear
as enchanting as a Willow Pattern plate.

85. —— *Lord of the East*. Cape, 1956. 15*s*.

An exciting adventure story, with a fictitious hero, but set in
China in the third century B.C., a background which is made real
and memorable.

86. GARNETT, R. S. *Unrecorded: a Tale of the Days of Chivalry*.
Benn, 1931.

From William Gregory's short account, in his *Chronicle of
London*, of how the Yorkist party sacked Ludlow in 1459 and
then 'robbyd the towne'.

87. GIELGUD, VAL. *Gathering of Eagles: a Story of 1812*. Constable, 1929.

If one can bear with a wildly improbable plot, this tale of
Napoleon's Russian campaign furnishes a superb picture of the
miseries and heroism of the famous retreat.

88. GOLDTHORPE, JOHN. *The Same Scourge*. Longmans, 1954.
12*s*. 6*d*.

The story of a Roman officer who studies the behaviour of
Christ and his Apostles, becomes converted to Christianity and
is finally a victim of the same scourge as Jesus.

89. GRAHAM, ALICE WALWORTH. *The Vows of the Peacock*. Eyre & Spottiswood, 1956. 16s.

An exciting and historically reliable first novel, depicting England in the first half of the fourteenth century—a period neglected by writers of historical fiction.

90. GRANT, JOAN. *Lord of the Horizon*. Methuen, 1943. 6s.

The author's third novel of Ancient Egypt. The story is not as thrilling as its predecessors (see 93, 94), but it has the same curious air of being an eye-witness account and is touched in places with real drama.

91. —— *Return to Elysium*. Methuen, 1947. 6s.

Lucina, a Greek girl, develops remarkable occult powers, in conflict with her mentor, Aesculapius. She goes to Rome, where she establishes herself as a priestess. The interest is brilliantly sustained, in a most impressive book.

92. —— *So Moses was Born*. Methuen, 1952. 6s.

A convincing picture of Ancient Egypt and its ruling caste, with an ingenious explanation to account for the finding of the baby Moses.

93. —— *Winged Pharoah*. Barker, 1937.

94. —— *Eyes of Horus*. Methuen, 1942.

The period of the First Dynasty in Egypt is superbly re-created in these two novels, almost as though the author were drawing upon the memory of a previous incarnation, and one can believe wholeheartedly in the stories. *Winged Pharoah*, in particular, is an example of the historical novel at its best.

95. GRAVES, ROBERT. *Count Belisarius*. Cassell, 1938. Penguin, 1956. 3s. 6d.

A striking reconstruction of the career, and final tragedy, of a figure of epic dimensions and great appeal. Belisarius was the Napoleon of the Age of Justinian, and a greater man than his master.

96. —— *Homer's Daughter*. Cassell, 1955. 10s. 6d.

Supposedly the memoirs of the Princess Nausicaa, daughter of King Alpheides of Aegesta in Sicily. There is a background of superstition, but the characters move and speak like real people. An earlier story of classical Greece by this author is *The Golden Fleece*, Cassell, 1944.

23

97. —— *I Claudius.* Barker, 1934. Penguin, 3*s.* 6*d.*

98. —— *Claudius the God and his Wife Messalina.* Barker, 1934. Penguin, 3*s.* 6*d.*

A critic called this work a reconstruction of the Julio-Claudians on the lines of the Forsyte Saga, and it certainly has the analytical approach of the latter. It is a most impressive study of the rise and subsequent decline and fall of the Emperor who conquered Britain. Volume I won both the Hawthornden and the James Tait Black Prizes for 1934.

99. —— *Sergeant Lamb of the Ninth.* Methuen, 1940.

100. —— *Proceed, Sergeant Lamb.* Methuen, 1941. 6*s.*

Sergeant Lamb was a real person who left the Army in 1784 and wrote his memoirs. The author has drawn upon these extensively for this absorbing picture of the British Army in the period of the American War of Independence.

101. GREEN, PETER. *Achilles his Armour.* Murray, 1955. 15*s.*

The life of Alcibiades in novel form, which incidentally gives a clear and accurate picture of fifth-century Greece, and the Peloponnesian War. The erudition at times lies heavily upon the story.

102. HARWOOD, ALICE. *Merchant of the Ruby.* Bodley Head, 1951. 12*s.* 6*d.*

An exciting and well-written tale. The Merchant of the Ruby is Perkin Warbeck, but the chief character is his wife, Catherine Gordon, cousin of the King of Scotland.

103. HERBERT, SIR A. P. *Why Waterloo?* Methuen, 1952. 6*s.*

Napoleon on Elba. A thrilling story and an excellent picture of the times. The nautical detail, in particular, is set out with the hand of a master.

104. HEYER, GEORGETTE. *The Conqueror.* Heinemann, 1931. 10*s.* 6*d.*

A long novel, based on the life of William, Duke of Normandy, from his birth in the house of a tanner of Falaise, to his coronation in Westminster Abbey.

105. —— *An Infamous Army.* Heinemann, 1937. 8*s.* 6*d.*

An outstanding novel of the 'Hundred Days', seen through the eyes of a group of aristocrats, civilians and soldiers assembled in

Brussels. The Waterloo campaign is made intelligible to the non-military reader.

106. —— *The Spanish Bride*. Heinemann, 1940. 8s. 6d.

A successful romance of the Peninsular War, in which the battles are lucidly described. The love story is a true one: that of Sir Henry Smith and his 'Spanish bride'.

107. IRWIN, MARGARET. *The Gay Galliard*. Chatto, 1941. 10s. 6d.

A violently partisan account of Mary, Queen of Scots. The gay galliard is Bothwell, but the figure of Mary holds the centre of the stage.

108. —— *Young Bess*. Chatto, 1944. 12s. 6d.

109. —— *Elizabeth, Captive Princess*. Chatto, 1948. 12s. 6d.

110. —— *Elizabeth and the Prince of Spain*. Chatto. 1953. 12s. 6d.

The story of Elizabeth Tudor. If the author can be faulted it is in the fact that she deals almost entirely in personalities. The great issues of the age are generally ignored.

111. —— *Royal Flush: the Story of Minette*. Chatto, 1932. 10s. 6d.

112. —— *The Proud Servant*. Chatto, 1934. 10s. 6d.

113. —— *Stranger Prince: the Story of Rupert of the Rhine*. Chatto, 1936. 12s. 6d.

114. —— *The Bride*. Chatto, 1939. 12s. 6d.

These four related novels are about certain people in the seventeenth century whose lives were linked together.

115. JEFFERIS, BARBARA. *Beloved Lady*. Dent, 1956. 15s.

The Paston Letters provide the material for what was described by a critic as 'a first-class historical novel, peopled with living characters'—England during the Wars of the Roses.

116. JENKINS, ELIZABETH. *The Phoenix Nest*. Gollancz, 1936.

A convincing picture of the Elizabethan Age in the years following the defeat of the Armada. We are in the world of the Elizabethan theatre—before the advent of Shakespeare—with Ned Alleyn, Henslowe and Christopher Marlowe.

117. JOHN, EVAN. *Crippled Splendour*. Nicholson & Watson, 1938.

James I, third king of the original house of Stewart, had one driving ambition: to lead the troubled Scotland of the fifteenth century back to the peace and prosperity of the golden age of two centuries earlier.

118. —— *Ride Home To-morrow: the Chronicle of a Crusader.* Heinemann, 1950.

The story of the last years of the Kingdom of Jerusalem, from the Christian point of view, in which Saladin is the arch enemy. It avoids the conventional happy ending and the almost equally conventional ending in failure and despair.

119. KAMBAN, GUDMUNDER. *I See a Wondrous Land.* Nicholson & Watson, 1938.

This novel by a distinguished Icelandic author is in the heroic mould—it tells of the colonisation of Greenland and the Norse discovery of America.

120. —— *The Virgin of Skalholt.* Nicholson & Watson, 1936.

A beautifully told story of Icelandic life in the seventeenth century.

121. KENYON, F. W. *Emma.* Hutchinson, 1955. 12*s.* 6*d.*

A 'cheerful, bustling, vivid tale'. It ends with the death of Nelson and the complicated financial settlement of his estate.

122. KING-HALL, MAGDALEN. *Gay Crusaders.* Peter Davies, 1934.

A brilliant reconstruction of mediaeval life in the years 1189–1192, the time of the Crusades. The story is in diary form and is told, in turn, by two English nobles and the two French ladies who entertain them.

123. KOESTLER, ARTHUR, *The Gladiators.* Cape, 1939.

The Gladiators' War, and the character of Spartacus, provide a superb theme for the historical novelist, and Mr. Koestler makes the most of it. Being also a political journalist, he draws parallels with the fateful years before the Second World War.

124. KRISLOV, ALEXANDER. *No Man Sings.* Longmans, 1956. 13*s.* 6*d.*

An unusually good first novel. Its theme is the life of Sappho—a difficult subject to portray successfully in view of the lack of source material.

125. LANCASTER, BRUCE. *Venture in the East*. Alvin Redman, 1952. 10s. 6d.

A first-class historical tale of adventure, which portrays the final closing of Old Japan to foreigners in the seventeenth century, and the bare survival of the Dutch East India Company.

126. LANE, JANE. *Come to the March*. Rich & Cowan, 1937.

Through the fortunes of the Lathom family, the author describes life in London under the Hanoverians during the years before the '45. She presents a careful and clever picture of a singularly unattractive period.

127. —— *England for Sale*. Andrew Dakers, 1943.

Much the same material as in her book *King James the Last*. Her portrait of James II as the one honest man in a world of bribery and cynicism is obviously partisan. But the general description of of the collapse of morals under the weight of corruption in high places is excellently done.

128. —— *Gin and Bitters*. Dakers, 1945.

England at the end of the seventeenth century, with a vivid picture of the City and the humble citizenry of London.

129. —— *London goes to Heaven*. Dakers, 1947.

The eleven years Interregnum. The author moves in that period with ease, showing the Republican episode as an unnatural un-English dictatorship.

130. —— *Prelude to Kingship*. Rich & Cowan, 1936.

This novel has no plot other than that provided by history, in itself one of the most romantic of all stories—that of Charles II. The portrait of Charles is first-class and the background is accurate and full of colour.

131. LE FORT, GERTRUD VON. *The Pope from the Ghetto*. Sheed & Ward, 1934.

Translated from the German, this is a historical novel well off the beaten track. Through the medium of a fictitious family we are given a dramatic and eminently successful study of the tumultuous struggle between Pope and Emperor in the twelfth century.

132. LESLIE, DORIS. *That Enchantress*. Hutchinson, 1954. 7s. 6d.

A study of Abigail Hill, the poor relation and protégée of the great Sarah, Duchess of Marlborough.

133. LINDSAY, JACK. *The Barriers are Down*. Gollancz, 1945.

The setting is Gaul during the break-up of the Roman Empire, and the story is of the fortunes of three sons of Roman land-owners.

134. —— *Hannibal Takes a Hand*. Dakers, 1941.

The year is 196 B.C. Carthage has been defeated in the Second Punic War and is burdened with a huge indemnity. In these circumstances Hannibal comes forward as the champion of the people against the Carthaginian oligarchy. This is a vivid, colour-ful and scholarly piece of work.

135. —— *Rome for Sale*. Elkin Mathews, 1934.

136. —— *Caesar is Dead*. Nicholson & Watson, 1934.

137. —— *Last Days with Cleopatra*. Nicholson & Watson, 1935.

The first volume of this trilogy represents the revolutionary movement in the last century of the Roman Republic; the second describes the religious impulse which produced 'Caesar-worship' and the third is concerned with the balance of forces which produced the Roman Empire out of the conflict. The emphasis is on imaginary characters, rather than the well-known historical figures, but the effect is brilliant and dramatic.

138. —— *The Wanderings of Wenamen*, 1115–1114 B.C. Nichol-son & Watson, 1936.

Probably the first historical novel to deal successfully with Ancient Egypt. The story is taken from a papyrus document preserved in Moscow, and the author paints a convincing picture of the 'decline and fall' of Egypt, with the growing power of Assyria menacing her on the horizon.

139. LINKLATER, ERIC. *Men of Ness*. Cape, 1932. 12s. 6d.

Once again the known facts are too few to allow a judgment on the historical accuracy of this novel of Viking life; but the broad effect is undoubtedly realistic—too much so for the squeamish. Mr. Linklater's Vikings lived the life of Hobbes's primitive man —'nasty, brutish and short'.

140. LOFTS, NORAH. *The Lute Player*. M. Joseph, 1951.

The lute-player is Blondel, the minstrel who discovered Richard Coeur de Lion in his dungeon, and the story is told by Blondel or by various ladies awaiting the return of their menfolk. Miss Lofts adopts a somewhat startling view of Richard's character, for which there is no historical evidence; but the vivid and accurate details make this an excellent tale of life in the twelfth century.

141. —— *The Road to Revelation.* Peter Davies, 1941. 10*s.* 6*d.*

Based on a famous and tragic episode in American history—the blazing of the trail across the desert into California in 1840.

142. MCGILL, HILDA MARY. *The Young Men Dream.* Heritage, 1934.

The struggle of the young Edward III to free himself from the domination of Isabella of France.

143. MACKENZIE, AGNES MURE. *Apprentice Majesty.* Serif Books, 1950.

A scholarly account of the twenty years between the death of Alexander III of Scotland and the crowning of Robert Bruce.

144. —— *Cypress in Moonlight.* Constable, 1931.

A fine study of an Italian ducal court at the end of the eighteenth century, when the exuberance of the Renaissance had become corrupt. Against this background is played the tragedy of the young Duchess—an exile from her native Brittany, married to a blasé Italian sensualist.

145. MADARIAGA, SALVADOR DE. *The Heart of Jade.* Collins, 1944. Cheap edn., 1956. 3*s.* 6*d.*

The Aztec civilisation and the clash with Spain.

146. MANN, HEINRICH. *King Wren.* Secker, 1937.

147. —— *Henri Quatre.* Secker, 1938.

148. —— *The Last Days of Henri Quatre.* Secker, 1939.

The life of Henry IV of France, depicted with a bold application of local colour and a fine sense of the dramatic elements in the story.

149. MANN, THOMAS. *Joseph and his Brothers.* Secker. 1956, 42*s.*

A re-issue in one volume of *Tales of Jacob* (1934), *The Young Joseph* (1935), *Joseph in Egypt* (1938) and *Joseph the Provider* (1944). This is an epic in which the biblical world is seen through the sharp eyes of the young Joseph, and every detail is reproduced with all the weight of archaeological evidence behind it. But the author steps out of the true line of historical novelists by giving his hero the mental attributes and perceptions of a man of the twentieth century.

150. MASEFIELD, JOHN. *Basilissa.* Heinemann, 1940. 8*s.* 6*d.*

The early story of the courtesan and actress Theodora, afterwards the wife of Justinian and Empress of the Eastern Empire. The setting is so vividly described that we feel almost as much at home in the streets of Constantinople as in those of our own neighbourhood.

151. —— *Conquer.* Heinemann, 1941.

A tail-piece to *Basilissa*—the story of the Nika Revolution when the struggle of the Greens and the Blues almost wrecked the City.

152. MASON, A. E. W. *Fire over England.* Hodder, 1936. 6*s.*

A dramatic tale of the war between England and the Spanish Inquisition.

153. —— *Königsmark.* Hodder, 1938. 6*s.*

The story of the young Swedish adventurer who was reputed to be the lover of the wife of George I. History is cleverly blended with imagination into a richly romantic story.

154. —— *Musk and Amber.* Hodder, 1942. 6*s.*

Venice of the eighteenth century, used as a colourful setting for a robust historical adventure story.

155. MASTERS, JOHN. *Nightrunners of Bengal.* M. Joseph, 1951. 15*s.*

Social life in a remote Bengal station at the time of the Indian Mutiny.

156. MITCHELL, JAMES L. (pseud.). *Spartacus.* Jarrolds, 1933.

The story of the great rising of the slaves in Southern Italy in 73 B.C., narrated in a direct style which is fast-moving and full of colour. It is a grim story, grimly told, but it is relieved by some good descriptions of scenery and setting. The characters of Spartacus, the leader of the revolt, and some of his lieutenants, are drawn in heroic proportions.

157. MITCHELL, MAIRIN. *The Odyssey of Acurio.* Heinemann, 1956. 16*s.*

The first voyage round the world—begun by Magellan and completed by Sebastian del Cano.

158. MITCHELL, MARY. *Birth of a Legend.* Methuen, 1956. 12*s.* 6*d.*

An exciting novel of intrigue in the Duchy of Brabant, in the tenth century, when Henry the Fowler was on his death-bed.

159. MITCHISON, NAOMI. *Cloud Cuckoo Land.* Cape, 1925.

The period is that of the Peloponnesian War, but this is used as a background, rich in detail, for real people to act out their lives in completely convincing surroundings.

160. —— *The Conquered.* Cape, 1923. 10s. 6d.

Caesar's *Gallic War*—re-told from the viewpoint of the Gauls, through the medium of the tragic life of a young Gallic chieftain. The author is faithful to the original sources, but she is at her best when she gives full rein to her imagination.

161. —— *The Corn King and the Spring Queen.* Cape, 1931. 15s.

One of the landmarks in the evolution of the historical novel. The setting is Scythia in the third century before Christ, and presents a panorama of the whole Aegean world.

162. MORLEY, IRIS. *Cry Treason.* Peter Davies, 1940.

A very readable account of the life and death of Monmouth. It contains an excellent study of Charles II.

163. —— *The Mighty Years.* Peter Davies, 1943.

The author's best work; a well-studied, realistic and vigorous portrait of William of Orange. Only one character is imaginary, Richard Wildman, representing the left-wing republicanism of the period.

164. —— *We Stood for Freedom.* Peter Davies, 1941.

Monmouth's Rebellion of 1685, as seen by some of its participants, in whom we can believe implicitly, and whose hopes and disappointments we can share.

165. MORRISON, LUCILE. *The Lost Queen of Egypt.* Secker, 1938.

Nefertiti is the queen, and this story of a great period of Egyptian civilisation is incredibly realistic in its reconstruction of life in Akhetaten, the city of flowers and peace. It is also a moving and beautiful love story.

166. MORROW, HONORÉ WILLSLIE. *Beyond the Blue Sierra.* Hutchinson, 1933.

A novel of action, with an unhackneyed theme—the opening up of California by Anza's expedition from Mexico, and the founding of that fabulous city, San Francisco.

167. —— *Let the King Beware.* Cassell, 1936.

The American Revolution, viewed from this side of the Atlantic.

The portraits of George III and Benjamin Franklin are exceptional creations.

168. —— *Yonder Sails the 'Mayflower'*. Hutchinson, 1935.

Dealing with the adventures of the Pilgrim Fathers in 1620, until they sailed for America, this is a valiant attempt to make the Puritan leaders appear human and likeable people.

169. MUNTZ, HOPE. *The Golden Warrior*. Chatto, 1948. 12s. 6d.

This very good novel is written in the style of a saga. It presents Harold and William the Conqueror as heroic characters, animated by uncomplicated but intense emotions. A multitude of episodes are all preludes to the climax of the Battle of Hastings.

170. MURRAY, D. L. *The Bride Adorned*. Constable, 1929.

The nineteenth-century clash between the Italian monarchy and the Pope, resulting in the end of the temporal power of the Papacy.

171. —— *Come like Shadows*. Hodder, 1955. 15s.

The theory of reincarnation is used for this interesting novel which displays a deep knowledge of revolutionary France.

172. —— *Commander of the Mists*. Hodder, 1938.

A tale of the '45, which, unlike the majority of historical novels on this theme, does not paint one side black and the other white. Probably the author's best book.

173. —— *Enter Three Witches*. Hodder, 1942. 9s. 6d.

London of the 'nineties', with all the atmosphere of this raffish and bohemian period, exposed through the story of Sam Rubens, old-clothes dealer, who becomes S. Macdermott Rubens, merchant in gold.

174. —— *Folly Bridge*. Hodder, 1945.

A novel of Oxford in the eighteenth century, with the emphasis on the rowdy and disreputable side of University life.

175. —— *Tale of Three Cities*. Hodder, 1940. 10s. 6d.

The three cities of this long, intricate and crowded story are Rome, London and Paris, between the years 1858 and 1871— from the attempt to assassinate Louis Napoleon to the Paris Commune.

176. —— *Trumpeter, Sound !* Hodder, 1933. 10s. 6d.

A historical novel with a Dickensian flavour, and of the Dickens period. Excitement in plenty is provided by the Crimean War, including the Charge of the Light Brigade and the legendary 'Apparition of the Unknown Mounted Soldier '.

177. NEILL, ROBERT. *Mist over Pendle*. Hutchinson, 1951. 7s. 6d.

A book which begins as an interesting account of London and Lancashire in the reign of James I, ends as something little better than a thriller. But despite its shortcomings, it is a well-written, exciting novel which gives an excellent account of daily life in the seventeenth century.

178. —— *Moon in Scorpio*. Hutchinson, 1952. 7s. 6d.

Another excellent historical thriller by this author, set in an accurate framework of the Popish Plot.

179. —— *Rebel Heiress*. Hutchinson, 1954. 7s. 6d.

The return of the exiled Cavaliers in 1660. In the words of one critic, this 'convincing and vivid book, written from a sound central position, makes past politics as exciting as the Cold War '.

180. NEUMANN, ALFRED. *The New Caesar*. Hutchinson, 1934.

181. —— *Man of December*. Hutchinson, 1937.

182. —— *The Friends of the People*. Hutchinson, 1941.

This trilogy of France of the Second Empire and the Third Republic almost escapes definition as a historical novel. It clings scrupulously to the facts, and the characters are all identifiable historical figures.

183. —— *The Patriot*. Peter Davies, 1929.

An exciting, fast-moving story of the assassination of Tsar Paul I by Count Pahlen, the Military Governor of St. Petersburg.

184. NEUMANN, ROBERT. *The Queen's Doctor*. Gollancz, 1936.

The doctor is one Johan Frederick Struensee, a fascinating and little-known figure who became the power behind the throne in Denmark during the reign of the boy king, Christian VII. Drama is furnished by the love affair of Struensee with the Queen-Consort, Caroline, the sister of George III.

185. —— *A Woman Screamed*. Cassell, 1938.

A theme which has a topical flavour: Hungary's revolt against the rule of Austria, and the revolution of 1848. The central figure is Kossuth, of whom someone said that he did more harm to the cause of Liberalism than anyone since Robespierre.

186. O'BRIEN, KATE. *That Lady*. Heinemann, 1946. *9s. 6d.*

A melodramatic story of high intrigue, set in the Spain of 1577–92. The world-shaking events of those years are dismissed in a few pages; the emphasis is on the character of Philip II and 'that lady'—Ana de Mendoza.

187. OLDENBOURG, ZOÉ. *The Corner-stone*. Gollancz, 1954. *7s. 6d.*

The author is a brilliant mediaevalist who exhibits a wonderful understanding of mediaeval psychology. She takes the reader back into the French way of life under Philippe le Bel, among the scholars, minstrels, pilgrims and crusaders who thronged the roads to the Holy Land.

188. —— *The World is not Enough*. Gollancz, 1949.

Another scholarly and imaginative reconstruction of France in the twelfth century, the period of the Third Crusade.

189. OLIVER, JANE. *Isle of Glory*. Collins, 1947.

The life of St. Columba, which gives a vivid impression of that extraordinary man, and of the foundation of what was to become the Kingdom of Scotland.

190. —— *The Lion is Come*. Collins, 1951. *6s.*

The story of Robert Bruce, showing evidence of wide reading on the subject. Scotsmen will enjoy it and Sassenachs can learn much from it.

191. —— *Sing, Morning Star*. Collins, 1949.

Did Malcolm live 'happily ever after', following his defeat of Macbeth? Miss Oliver picks up Malcolm's story at a point in time just before that at which Shakespeare laid it down. Her theme is the conflict between the tempestuous Malcolm and his queen, the gentle Margaret.

192. —— *Sunset at Noon*. Collins, 1955.

James IV of Scotland was a most able monarch, and the author brings all her knowledge, imagination and sympathy to bear in presenting a lively picture of this attractive figure of the Renaissance.

193. OMAN, CAROLA. *The Best of his Family.* Hodder, 1933. 12s. 6d.

Shakespeare, Southampton and 'The Dark Lady'. Immortal Will lives in these pages, and so do the members of his family—Anne, John Shakespeare, Judith—and his friends, particularly John Burbage.

194. —— *Crouchback.* Hodder, 1929. 12s. 6d.

The author knows the history of the fifteenth century well, and she tries to present a less distasteful picture of Richard than that with which we are familiar; but she is fighting a losing battle against Shakespeare and Sir Laurence Olivier.

195. —— *The Empress.* Hodder, 1932.

A sympathetic study of the Empress Maud, until her declining years as Regent of Normandy, with her son Henry on the English throne and her grandsons playing at her knee. The spotlight is always on Maud, but the historical figures surrounding her are not shadows.

196. —— *Major Grant.* Hodder, 1931.

The Peninsular War, from a different angle. The hero is Wellington's Chief Intelligence Officer, and the action takes place in the Paris of 1812. The result is a spy story, with an authentic setting.

197. —— *Over the Water.* Hodder, 1935.

The familiar story of Prince Charles Edward and Flora Macdonald, against a background which is a superb piece of historical reconstruction.

198. —— *The Road Royal.* Unwin, 1924.

The author's first novel. A study of Mary Stuart which shows her neither as Swinburne's 'diamond heart unflawed and clear' nor as Maurice Hewlett's romantic figure.

199. O'NEILL, JOSEPH. *Chosen by the Queen.* Gollancz, 1947.

The last years of Elizabeth's reign, and the fall of Essex, seen through the eyes of one of his minor clerks. The portrait of the Queen in her haunted and unhappy old age is good; but even more interesting is the bustling picture of life in a great sixteenth-century household.

200. —— *Wind from the North.* Cape, 1934.

A study of everyday life in the eleventh-century Norse town of Dyflin, which today is Dublin. A fine story with an unusual and little-known background.

201. ONIONS, OLIVER. *Arras of Youth.* M. Joseph, 1949.

The history of Robert Gandelyn, clerk, soldier, actor, and spy, unfolded in the troubled and unhappy setting of fifteenth-century Yorkshire. The author has a deep knowledge of the declining Middle Ages and a profound feeling for the spirit of the times.

202. —— *A Penny for the Harp.* M. Joseph, 1952.

The plot turns on the conflict between Welsh and English law along the Welsh Marches, in the fifteenth century. This is a beautifully written story which presents a perfectly credible picture of a vanished way of life.

203. —— *Poor Man's Tapestry.* M. Joseph, 1946.

Life among the common people during the Wars of the Roses; the author exhibits a remarkable wealth of knowledge of the husbandry, the crafts and the customs of the fifteenth century.

204. —— *The Story of Ragged Robin.* M. Joseph, 1945.

The major events of history do not figure in this novel of the seventeenth century, but it gives a wonderful impression of every-day life and speech in that age, together with a superb plot.

205. OWEN, CUNLIFFE. *The Phoenix and the Dove.* Rich & Cowan, 1933.

A study of 'Mr. W. H.', who is identified with the Earl of Southampton. The passions which moved Shakespeare, Queen Elizabeth and the Dark Lady of the Sonnets are depicted with great skill.

206. PETERSEN, NIS. *The Street of the Sandalmakers.* Lovat Dickson, 1932.

In this story of Rome in the age of Marcus Aurelius, few major historical characters appear; the setting is in the back streets of the city, where hucksters rub shoulders with priests and philosophers. Historians may raise their eyebrows in places, but the general effect is very convincing.

207. PICK, ROBERT. *The Escape of Socrates.* Chatto, 1955. 15s.

For readers who do not know the story of Socrates, this will be a suspense novel. Others will be intrigued by the detailed description of the topography of ancient Athens and the procedure used in its law courts.

208. PILGRIM, DAVID. *No Common Glory.* Macmillan, 1942. 6s.

209. —— *The Grand Design.* Macmillan, 1944.

Two novels which recount the story of the mysterious figure of James de la Cloche, the natural son of Charles II, who flashed like a meteor across the sky of Restoration diplomacy.

210. —— *So Great a Man.* Macmillan, 1937.

In 1808–9 Napoleon was at the height of his power, but the seeds of his ultimate destruction were already being sown. The book is written in the episodic style of a film scenario, which gives it tremendous pace.

211. PLAIDY, JEAN. *Madame Serpent.* Hale, 1951. 10s. 6d.

212. —— *The Italian Woman.* Hale, 1952. 10s. 6d.

213. —— *Queen Jezebel.* Hale, 1953. 10s. 6d.

A trilogy devoted to the life of Catherine de Medici, who, married when a girl of 15, spent twenty years as a passive, neglected wife and then developed into the sinister woman known to history.

214. —— *St. Thomas's Eve.* Hale, 1954.

This is a charming picture of the life and death of Sir Thomas More.

215. —— *The Sixth Wife.* Hale, 1953.

An absorbing and accurate life of a minor figure who touched great events—Katherine Parr, who outlived Henry VIII to marry the man she had always loved.

216. POWYS, JOHN COWPER. *Owen Glendower.* Lane, 1942.

A gigantic novel written round the Welsh rising under Owen Glendower, at the beginning of the fifteenth century.

217. PREEDY, GEORGE R. (pseud.). *Laurell'd Captains.* Hutchinson, 1935.

Deals with the early part of the French revolution, and contains some excellent scenes depicting the mingled horror and excitement of those epoch-making days.

218. —— *My Tattered Loving.* Jenkins, 1937.

An account of the celebrated 'Overbury Mystery' of the reign of James I. The author keeps to the facts, but puts an individual interpretation upon them.

219. —— *Primula.* Hodder, 1940.

A rare type of historical novel which is also a crime story, set in the early days of the French Revolution.

220. —— *The Rocklitz.* Bodley Head, 1930.

A vivid illumination of one of the dark corners of history—Saxony after the Thirty Years War. 'The Rocklitz' was Margaretta Sybilla Von Neitschutz, born in poverty, but destined to become the power behind the throne of Saxony.

221. —— *Tumult in the North.* Bodley Head, 1931.

A tale of the Rising of '15. The author blends fact and fancy in a most skilful manner.

222. PRESCOTT, H. F. M. *The Lost Fight.* Constable, 1928.

Mediaeval France, but a generation later than that of the author's first historical novel—*The Unhurrying Chase.* The characters are real people, men and women of their time, not translated from our own age.

223. —— *The Man on a Donkey.* Eyre & Spottiswoode, 1952. 18*s.*

One of the great historical novels of our time; a magnificent reconstruction of the living past, the fruit of years of work by a learned hstorian who is also a novelist of considerable stature. The main theme is the Pilgrimage of Grace, in the reign of Henry VIII.

224. —— *Son of Dust.* Constable, 1932.

The conflict between human and divine love; the setting is England in the early eleventh century, before the Norman invasion. The background is slowly drawn, with infinite care, and becomes a world in which the reader can believe.

225. —— *The Unhurrying Chase.* Eyre & Spottiswoode, 1925. 15*s.*

The title is taken from Francis Thompson's 'The Hound of Heaven' and the struggle between earthly love and ambition and the love of God is superbly worked out in the period of the twelfth century, where one of the central characters is Richard Coeur de Lion.

226. RAYNOLDS, ROBERT. *The Sinner of Saint Ambrose.* Secker, 1953.

An exciting story and a vivid reconstruction of the past, this is the imaginary life of Julian, a lieutenant of Stilicho, the barbarian general who defended Rome against Alaric, in the fifth century.

227. RENAULT, MARY. *The Last of the Wine.* Longmans, 1956. 16*s*.

The life story of Alexias, an Athenian of good family, born at the beginning of the Peloponnesian War.

228. ROBERTS, B. DEW. *The Island Feud.* Chatto, 1947.

Here we are in Anglesey, during the Civil War. Richard Cheadle and his wife are on trial for the murder of her first husband, ten years earlier. With this dramatic centre-piece is woven the story of some of the humbler folk of the island. The book has a quiet, elegant style.

229. ROBERTS, KENNETH. *Arundel: a Chronicle of the Province of Maine and of the Secret Expedition against Quebec.* Bodley Head, 1936. 5*s*.

The plot is uninspired, but the background is superbly painted and in itself almost a *raison d'être* for the book, while the account of the attack on Quebec is a brilliant piece of writing.

230. —— *Lydia Bailey.* Collins, 1947. 3*s*. 6*d*.

The story of Lydia contributes little more than the title to the book. The author is far more interested in the setting—the Negro republic in Haiti during the Napoleonic period.

231. —— *Northwest Passage.* Collins, 1938. Cheap edn., 1953. 4*s*.

The New World, just before the American Revolution. The characterisation of Major Robert Rogers, and the story of his march on the French settlement, are equal to anything in historical fiction. Unfortunately, this high quality is not sustained to the end of the book, although it remains interesting and very readable.

232. —— *Oliver Wiswell.* Collins, 1943.

The American Revolution, with a difference. The hero is a loyalist and the rebels are regarded as the forces of evil.

233. —— *Rabble in Arms.* Collins, 1939.

The hero is Benedict Arnold, who is regarded by every American schoolboy as the personification of black treachery. To Mr. Roberts he is a leader of men, great in ability and in soul.

Considered simply as an adventure story this is first-class, but it is also a brilliant historical novel.

234. ROXBURGH, R. A. *Robin Bide-a-wee*. Blackwood, 1928.

Scotland of the Highlands in the later Jacobite days. From the point of view of style, setting, local colour and authentic atmosphere this is in the front rank.

235. SCARFOGLIO, CARLO. *The True Cross*, 1177–1192. Gollancz, 1956. 15s.

A remarkable novel about the last years of the Kingdom of Jerusalem. The story of Guido, who was moved to serve the Cross in the ranks of the Knights Templars, and was subsequently disillusioned, moves at tremendous speed against an authentic background which is never intrusive.

236. SELLICK, G. GODFRAY. *A Poor Man came in Sight*. Hodder, 1930.

England in the age of Wyclif. The author has the ability to write English which suggests the fourteenth century without either needing a glossary or sounding like a fancy dress ball.

237. SETTLE, MARY LEE. *O Beulah Land*. Heinemann, 1956. 18s.

The first of four novels destined to recount the making of the American nation. The setting is the author's native Virginia, 1754–74, and the theme is the westward move of the early pioneers towards the Ohio.

238. SHEEAN, VINCENT. *A Day of Battle*. Hamish Hamilton, 1938.

The day is 11 May 1745, and the battle is Fontenoy. The scene hardly shifts from the battlefield, but the novel has life and vigour and does full justice to the glory of the Irish Brigade that day.

239. SHEPPARD, ALFRED TRESSIDER. *Brave Earth*. Cape, 1925.

The Reformation, seen through the eyes of ordinary folk. The setting is the West Country where the revolt of 1549 against the new Prayer Book first began. A noble and moving story.

240. —— *The King's Goose*. Hodder, 1931.

The court and kingdom of Louis XII and Francis I of France, depicted in great detail with all the pageantry, colour and cruelty of the age.

241. —— *The Matins of Bruges*. Butterworth, 1938.

John Battle, son of a Winchelsea seaman, is the peg on which hangs this story of the rivalry of England and France in the thirteenth century, and the struggle of Flanders to escape from French domination.

242. —— *Queen Dick*. Hodder, 1929.

The theme is the failure of Richard Cromwell, the Protector's son, who proved so lamentably small for his father's shoes; but the book is brought to life by 'Old Noll' who storms through its pages like a whirlwind.

243. —— *Rome's Gift*. Hodder, 1936.

The Papacy during the fourteenth century—the period of the Great Schism. The accumulation of detail is triumphantly successful.

244. SHEPPARD, ALFRED TRESSIDER, and MACLEOD, RODERICK *A Rose for Scotland*. Hodder, 1933.

The theme—the marriage of Margaret Tudor, daughter of Henry VII, and King James IV of Scotland—is handled in lively fashion. The account of Margaret's journey to Scotland is a remarkable piece of historical description.

245. SIMON, EDITH. *The Chosen*. Bodley Head, 1940.

The story of Moses, told by the princess who rescued him from the banks of the Nile.

246. —— *The Golden Hand*. Cassell, 1952. 12s. 6d.

Among the glories of the Middle Ages, and a priceless legacy to us, were the great cathedrals. This entertaining and remarkable story is a description of the building of a fictitious cathedral in East Anglia, on a spot where a miraculous hand had been discovered. The task of building is spread over fifty years and is interrupted by the Black Death and the Peasant's Revolt.

247. *The Twelve Pictures*. Cassell, 1956. 15s.

The Nibelungenlied re-told in the light of modern psychology, as a dream of wish-fulfilment; but the book is not as difficult as that makes it appear. The picture of the barbarian world is convincing and the characters who enact the dramatic story are drawn in the round.

248. SIMPSON, HELEN. *Boomerang*. Heinemann, 1932.

A vivid description of Australia at three different periods—about 1837, in the 70's and around 1900. Though impressionistic, these sketches make a first-class contribution to our understanding of Australian social and political life.

249. —— *Saraband for Dead Lovers*. Heinemann, 1935.

The tragedy of Sophia-Dorothea of Zelle, wife of the future George I, and her lover Königsmark.

250. —— *Under Capricorn*. Heinemann, 1937.

A romantic story with a background of the early development of Australia in the 1830's.

251. SINCLAIR, UPTON. *Manassas*. Laurie, 1933.

The period is that leading up to the American Civil War, and the historical characters—Lincoln, Jefferson Davis, John Brown—blend easily with the fictitious elements of the story.

252. STEEN, MARGUERITE. *The Sun is my Undoing*. Collins, 1941. 18s.

History is drawn slightly larger than life in this colourful story of Bristol and the slave trade; it ranges from eighteenth-century Bristol to the Gold Coast, Cuba, Spain and back to Bristol. It is the first volume of a trilogy which follows the fortunes of the Flood family up to the present time. The other volumes are *Twilight on the Floods* and *Phoenix Rising*.

253. STEWART, GEORGE R. *Last of the Giants*. Harrap, 1939.

The early history and development of California—from the Mexican settlers to the gold prospectors from the East.

254. SUTCLIFF, ROSEMARY. *Lady in Waiting*. Hodder, 1956. 13s. 6d.

The lady in waiting was the wife of Sir Walter Raleigh, but the core of the book is the three-cornered conflict between Essex, Robert Cecil and Raleigh. The author successfully conveys the tense atmosphere of the ceaseless struggle for court favour.

255. THANE, ELSWYTH. *Young Mr. Disraeli*. Constable, 1937.

All the characters are historical, and both they and the events of their time are brilliantly evoked.

256. TREECE, HENRY. *The Dark Island*. Gollancz, 1952.

A good study of Celtic Britain in the first century; but it would have been very much better if the author had made his characters something more than puppets in historical costume. In spite of this, it is well worth reading.

257. —— *The Great Captains*. Bodley Head, 1956. 13s. 6d.

A vivid novel of Dark Age Britain, in which Arthur and his Knights are stripped of their glamour and shown as barbarous

Celtic war-leaders. A historian-critic contends that it contains historical blunders, but these will probably only worry the student of the period.

258. TREVOR, MERIOL. *The Last of Britain.* Macmillan, 1956. 16s.
On the scanty documentary evidence of sixth-century Britain which is still extant, the author has built a concrete and convincing world round Bath, Gloucester and Cirencester.

259. TROUNCER, MARGARET. *Madame Elisabeth.* Hutchinson, 1955. 12s. 6d.
The sister of Louis XVI of France gives her name to a scholarly and interesting account of the Court of Versailles.

260. UNDSET, SIGRID. *Kristin Lavransdatter.* Knopf, 1930.
A saga of life in fourteenth-century Norway. One of the really great historical novels.

261. VINOGRADOV, ANATOLII. *The Black Consul.* Gollancz, 1935.
The story of Toussaint L'Ouverture and the revolt of San Domingo, set against the background of the French Revolution.

262. WADDELL, HELEN. *Peter Abelard.* Constable, 1933. 12s. 6d.
The author of *The Wandering Scholars* is obviously at home in the age of the mediaeval schoolmen, and she brings her knowledge and her great delight in the period to bear upon the immortal story of Heloise and Abelard.

263. WALPOLE, SIR HUGH. *The Bright Pavilions.* Macmillan, 1940. 12s. 6d.
In general, the well-known 'Herries' novels can hardly be classed as historical fiction; but this chapter in the saga is an exception. Nicholas and Robin Herries are the central characters in an adventure story of Elizabethan England.

264. WALTARI, MIKA. *The Dark Angel.* Putnam, 1953. 12s. 6d.
A story of the last siege of Constantinople, in 1453. Exhibiting a complete mastery of the sources, this is the author's best book to date.

265. —— *Michael the Finn.* Putnam, 1950. 12s. 6d.
A picaresque novel of the sixteenth century; its setting is far wider than Finland—it also takes in Germany, the Near East and Rome.

43

266. —— *Sinuhe the Egyptian.* Putnam, 1949. 15s.

This long novel is in autobiographical form, the narrator being an Egyptian born in the same year as Akhenaton (c. 1400 B.C.). It is a wonderful feat of 'back-projection' into a distant era.

267. —— *The Sultan's Renegade.* Putnam, 1951.

A sequel to *Michael the Finn*. From the sack of Rome in 1527 the hero samples captivity in Tunis, is converted to the Islamic faith, and becomes involved in the wars of Suleiman the Magnificent. Every character is an utter rogue, but some of them are most likeable scoundrels.

268. WARNER, SYLVIA TOWNSEND. *The Corner that Held Them.* Chatto, 1948. 10s. 6d.

A rambling but witty and charming book depicting the life of the nuns in the fourteenth-century convent at Oby.

269. WHITE, STEWART EDWARD. *The Long Rifle.* Hodder, 1932.

A superb novel of the pioneering days of the far west of the United States, which was opened up by fur trappers and traders who unwittingly conquered a continent.

270. WILDER, THORNTON. *The Ides of March.* Longmans, 1948. 9s. 6d.

A short, witty, but extremely serious, work which contains no narrative or dialogue. The book is made up of letters, memoranda and fragments of verse—'a fantasia on certain events and persons of the last days of the Roman Republic'.

271. WILLIAMS, JAY. *The Good Yeomen.* Macdonald, 1956. 15s.

England in the fourteenth century, not Merrie England, for the emphasis is on the seamy side of life. The story is of Robin Hood, depicted as an outlawed gentleman whose object is to regain his heritage.

272. —— *The Siege.* Macdonald, 1955. 12s. 6d.

The Siege of Carcassonne in the Albigensian Crusade, the chief characters being the Provençal knights who pillaged their fellow-countrymen in the name of religion. An excellent picture of the 'age of chivalry'.

273. WILLIAMS, PATRY (pseud.) *God's Warrior.* Faber, 1942.

The two writers who collaborated so successfully under this pseudonym in *I am Canute* also took the Anglo-Saxon period for the scene of their second novel. The Christian soldier is

44

Dunstan, the architect of Church and State for almost half a century. But the theme lacks the drama of their first effort.

274. —— *I am Canute.* Faber, 1938.

Displays all the colour, cruelty and courage of the eleventh-century struggle between Saxons and Danes.

275. WILLIAMSON, HUGH ROSS. *Captain Thomas Schofield.* Collins, 1942.

A fictional attempt to answer the historical riddle of why, in the few months between July, 1647, and October, 1648, Oliver Cromwell changed from a staunch believer in the eventual restoration of Charles I into an implacable regicide.

276. WYDENBRUCK, NORA. *Placidia's Daughter.* Lehmann, 1952. 12*s.* 6*d.*

A fine example of the historical novel, with ordinary fictitious people placed easily and naturally in a setting, of stormy fifth-century Italy.

277. YEO, MARGARET. *King of Shadows.* Sheed & Ward, 1929.

The king is the luckless son of James II, who spent his life in exile on the Continent. The intrigues, colour and violence of this episode of history provide Miss Yeo with a highly dramatic plot.

278. YOUNG, FRANCIS BRETT. *They Seek a Country.* Heinemann, 1937. 15*s.*

The Great Trek of the Cape Dutch away from English rule in South Africa, written from the Afrikander viewpoint. Ignoring its bias, the novel offers excellent descriptions of the country and of the life of the migrants.

279. YOURCENAR, MARGUERITE. *Memoirs of Hadrian.* Secker, 1955. 15*s.*

One of the most remarkable historical novels to have appeared for many years; its author is reputed to have been working on it since 1924. Its blend of learning, psychological feeling for the spirit of these remote days, and the impeccable style, which has not been spoiled by translation from the French, should ensure for this book a lasting place among the great historical novels of this or any age.

SUBJECT INDEX

THE ANCIENT WORLD

THE DARK AGES

THE MIDDLE AGES

THE MAKING OF MODERN EUROPE

THE EXPANSION OF BRITAIN

THE NEW WORLD

www.ingramcontent.com/pod-product-compliance
Ingram Content Group UK Ltd.
Pitfield, Milton Keynes, MK11 3LW, UK
UKHW020448010325
455719UK00015B/475

9 781107 622135